Gravity

An Earthy Exploration
of the Metaphysical

J. Esther Goldthwaite

ISBN 978-0-578-62118-0

Illustrations by T. Quinn Kirkham.

To all those I know and love
and for the weary soul.

- E.G.

Dedicated to my sister and
her faith in my work.

- T.Q.K.

Contents

Introduction 7

Gravity 11

Moments 13

Living Water 15

Loss 17

A Winter's Dawn 19

Sunshower—Schmerzensreich 21

Sunrise 23

Compassion 25

Ariadne 27

To Nurture My Soul 29

Hope of My Heart 33

I Am 35

Fragments 37

Moonlight 39

Necessity.. 41

Forgiveness... 43

Home... 45

Introduction

Ideas have shapes:[1]

Loneliness sits in an empty space. Judgement splits like a singing sword. Love breathes in an embrace. When I meet with shapes without, I meet with shapes within; I sense the soul's substance and feel the forms of eternity. This is the beauty of poetry.

Poetry is more than arbitrarily chosen rhymes and rhythms. Poetry, including her rhymes and rhythms, is metaphor—is the joining of spirit and form. It is in moments when I realize this sacred union between the things I sense and the sense of those things that the seed of a poem lodges in my soul.

I'll sit by a stream under the sun and think, 'The fragmented reflection of light on the disturbed surface of the brook mirrors the fragmented reflection of truth on the disturbed soul.' The cadence of the words break with the broken flow of the broken brook and the broken soul, in contrast with the words recorded in this sentence. The sound of the single word, light, holds the sudden crescendo and crackle of a growing ember and that swift expansion that clicks into place when truth is realized. This is how my poems are born.

---

1 Similar to the Renaissance conception of rhetorical style as both presentation and embodiment of thought through similarity of form as discussed by Nancy Christiansen, I propose that shapes and entities in nature are governed by the same or similar "laws" as abstractions in human thoughts. (Christiansen, Nancy L. Figuring Style: The Legacy of Renaissance Rhetoric. University of South Carolina Press. 2013, pp. 1-33)

Shapes hold ideas.

J. Esther Goldthwaite

Gravity

When falls one foot to earth to cling to Earth—
That massive globe of glistening fruit, which hangs
In bowers midst the silky space where soft
And deepening shadows glint with fire cut Gems—
We fall, from where we were to where we are
To fall to where our souls have yet to be.

We crawl, we walk, we dance, we traverse Earth—
The weight of Substance tying threads from form
To form, like ligaments of secret Sight,
To gather up existence into life—

Moments

Moments—
When the fingers cling
To a crumbling hold
And grasp the blank abyss...

Moments—
When the chest heaves
With the weeping weight
Of the silent Nothing...

Moments—
When the heart trembles
Like a crinkled leaf
And shivers against the expansive sky...

Moments...
When the eyes blink
At the stinging brilliance
Of the deaths that hold rebirth—

Living Water

Earth peered through a dusty veil
Towards a barren, bone bleached sky.
Swiftly, a sudden spark sang deeply,
Over the heat beaten soil.

Softening and brightening,
Colors collected shades of vibrancy
Under the silver beads of a darkened sky.

Tears tumble in silver streams,
Trembling, but with a joyous laughter
To spill strength into plain parched earth.

Life lifted from burdened breath,
Quickened earth looks up to embrace
The quieting warmth of a singing dawn.

Loss

My grief is like a hollow stone
Where dripping waters slowly slink,
Then running, slip from leaf to fire
Encrusted leaf to drop into
The void and tap its cupping heart.

It lives where softly plinking rain
Descends in tiny stings and slides
Across the blank, unmoving face
Of shadow stained, impassive rock
That dimples cold and clammy clay.

My swimming eyes can hardly hold
Those rocky scenes and dream filled trees
Which, soaked in sunbeam yesterday,
Lie silent in the drizzled grey
Of flooding fogs and memories.

A Winter's Dawn

A gleaming glow
Through mists and snow
Is song in sight
—Heavn's fiery light—

For though
Winds whisper dread
And cold,
A warmth is spread
Through eyes to soul
That fills, like bread,
A hunger low.

Sunshower—Schmerzensreich

When walking from your door today...
The dewy fingers of lilting rains,
    Descending,
        Stroked the springing grass
    And plucked the weeping leaves
Beneath the Sunlight's cloudless eves.

Soft, sweeping through the sunlit space,
    Her teary veil, with solemn grace,
        Caught gently in the sparkling,
    Dancing,
Laughing light she cradled in her azure eyes,
Augmented through that glistening Sight.

Sunrise

Stars' silvery pins, 'neath blankets black,
Pierce shades of violet, pushing back
To lift those dim and velvet sheets
That veil the face of Heaven's Heat.

Soft sapphire hues—the hints of day—
Are seeping through a mist of grey.
Then tinged with rose—the morning's bud—
There blushes bright the Daylight's blood.

Its flickering flames of crimson crack
Night's darkening shades and peel them back—
So shrinking small, the twilight dim
Will crumble, sinking, folding in—
Till fold on fold,
Red burns to gold,
And Darkness must release its hold.

Compassion

I see that hollow haunting
In the chambers of your eyes
And I've felt that horror
Of death that dwells within
The breathing, sensing form—
Hope's embers sitting silent;
Pain's pallor on the sunken soul.
Deadened stones and steel
Seem softer by solidity; more real.

...

Can one spark of living light
Shine through my eyes
To liven you?

Ariadne

Two tethered lines entangle in
the chambers of my heart.
I feel the tension of the chords;
The tug from ties at ends not seen.

One rope rambles in
a swaying, sighing pull,
As though it were tied to the tides
Of the rising and falling sea,
Or to a ship adrift in her uncertainty.

The other, constant—as fixed
As the polar star, and as distant—
Leading on, and yet on, no nearer
For struggle; yet I've come much farther
By its ever present pull.

Two tethered lines entangle in
The chambers of my heart.
I feel the tension of the chords;
The tug from ties at ends not seen.

To Nurture My Soul

In isolated hours of reflection,
Shrouded in memory
As in veils of elusive night,
I heard a shrill
        but solemn cry
Weeping under the heavens.

Her voice was the voice of a child,
And she spoke from chambers
Buried deep inside my soul:
"Hold me! Oh, hold me!"

It was a simple yet sacred cry—
the plaintive infant's plea
That sleeps in the root
of every being—
The cry for the womb-like arms
Of Love.

As my soul has traveled and fallen
In barren lands,
This child's voice
Has pierced each passing way.

Waking,
as from a sleepless dream,
I lift her up and wrap her in my arms.

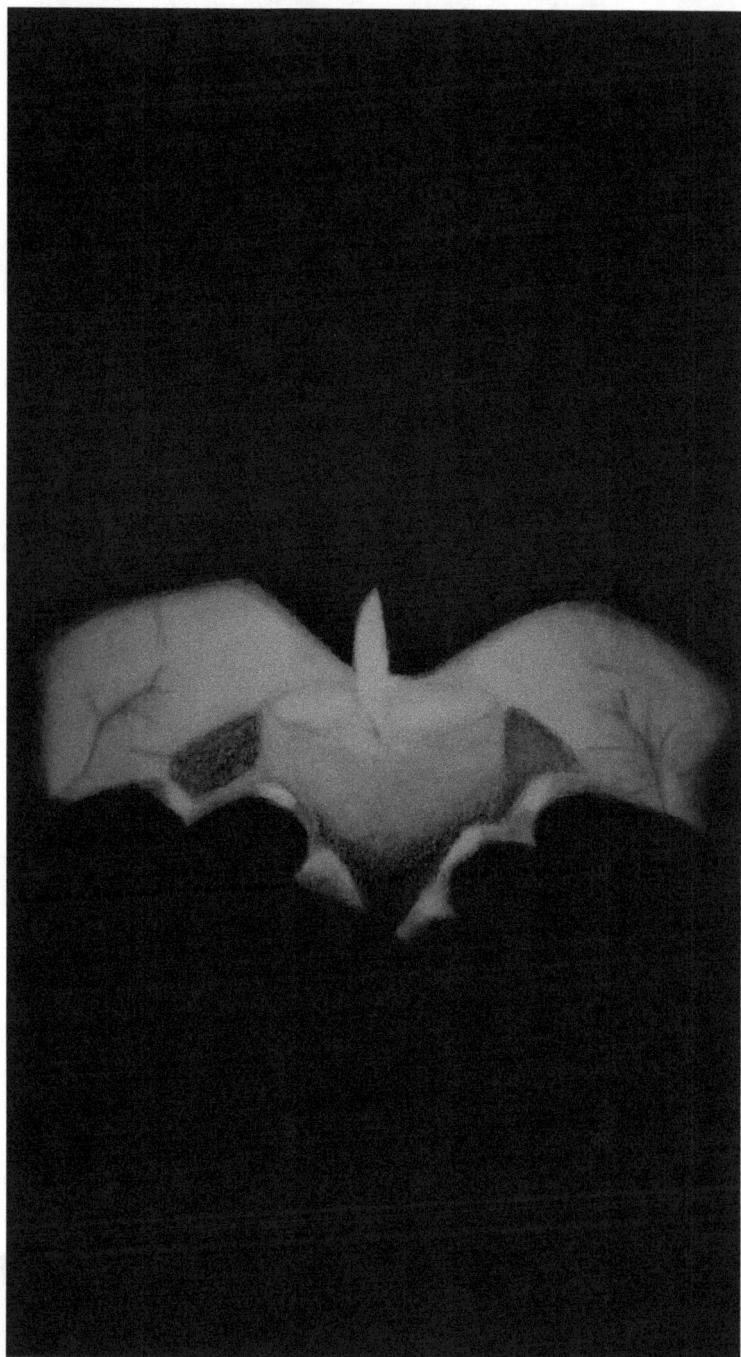

I carry her beneath a ledge
Of glistening, granite stone
And warm her with a flame of unseen light.

Cradling her,
I sing softly into a storm.
My breath whispers
Into the sweeping
Torrents of ice
To gild them
Warmly
With haunting hopes that flower
In the bosom of my child
        and sleep,
                In golds and greens,
Beneath the winter's whitewashed waves.

Here,
Yes here and now,
I will breathe fresh life into the frozen earth.

Hope of My Heart

A springing green creeps soft and slow
And silent, peers through bony boughs,

While inward, ringing, rumbles loud--
A triumph drumming in the cloud.

That joyful throbbing of the heart
Engorges what was dead with life;

Yes, all that slumbered 'gainst the dark
Awakes and shakes off dreams of strife.

They scatter with the morning dew;
I breathe in hopes of love anew.

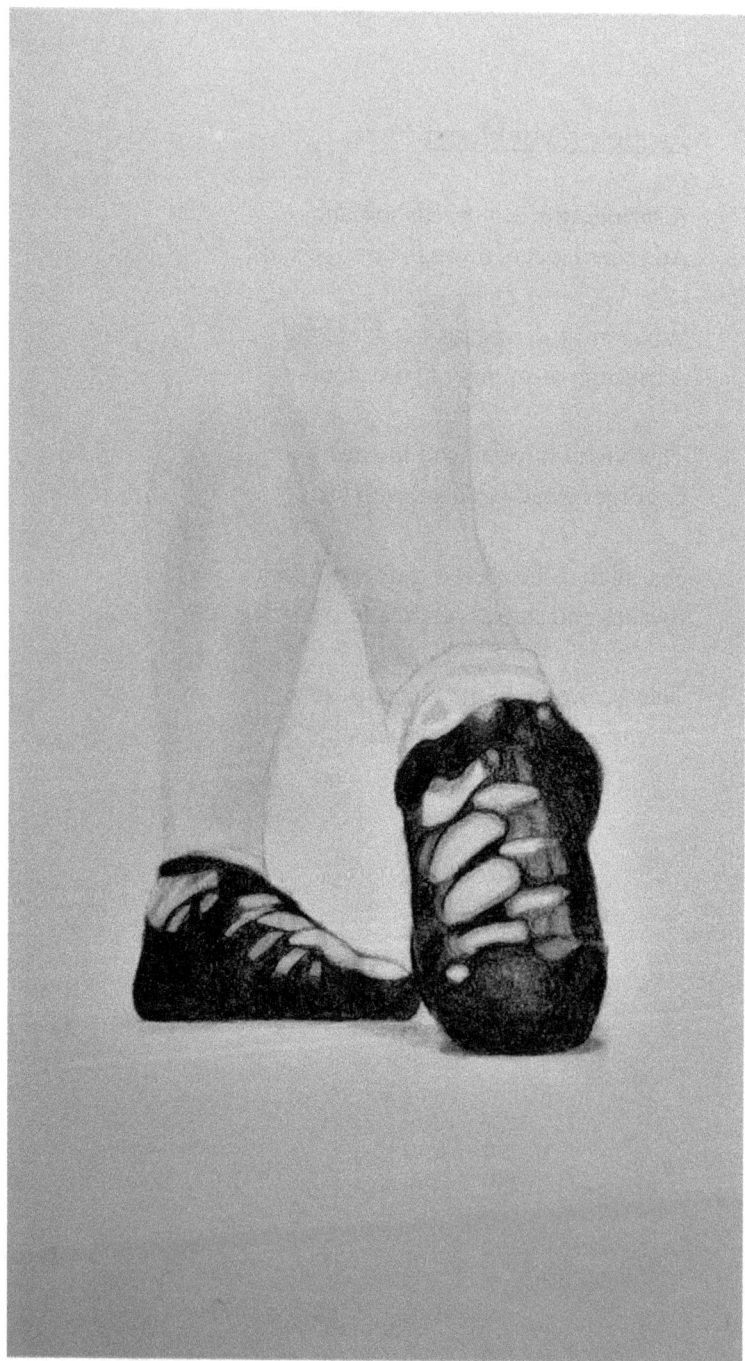

I Am

Let me sing.
Let me dance.
Let my heart and feet beat
In unison to the pattern
Of things Untold.

Let me play.
Why would I cram my soul
Into my hand
Or into my tongue
To speak dead nonsense?

Why must I make sense
To you?
Is it not enough
To make sense to myself
And to the earth beneath my feet?

Why must you wring me dry
Of meaning,
Till my spirit is parched
As bleached bone,
'To find out what I really mean?'

Fragments

The rushing steps
        Of a stumbling Stream
Tumbled on a
           Jagged rock,
     Falling
With a Face that wrinkled
    On the thorn-like edge
           And broke bright beams
              In its flitting eyes,
                  Reflecting
          The Light
          In
                Shattered
           Fragments.

Moonlight

Silence washes the soul
With music of an echoed light—
The light that seeps into the breast
When—of a sudden—all is
Still.

Necessity

When emerald melts to crimson
In the fingers of the Oak,
He drops his jewels one by one
As each one shrivels into smoke.

As night descends like leaking ink,
His bare hands weave the empty space
Between his Bones that—reaching—link
To catch the starlight in their place.

Forgiveness

The winter's slowly wafting dust—
The frost—
Is sighing through the silence,
Ornamenting living breath
With tiny, frozen tears that drift,
Like Shades of stones,
And settle on my dampened soul
That—with the soil—
Is chilled to stiffened clay.

My gaze drifts up—
As snow drifts down—
Through mini cloths of softened light
That flutter through the feathered winds
From Wings that spread beyond the sight—
To slowly wash the smoke-stained air
And blanket bare and shivering soil.

Beneath its warmth of icy down,
I drink its melting Sacrament
And shoot new tendrils of my soul
Between the breathing, thawing stones
To softly clothe the loosened soil.

Home

Where shadows sob against the light
In windy shreds of sweeping sighs,
Then shudder
With relief
And laughter
As their breaking Sorrow soaks the fields
For gratitude in Plenty's yield—

Where piercing pines are
Stretching in the pungent gloom,
And spice the
Dampened dust
Like a breathing rust
That tingles with the Christmas scent
Of a Promise that is meant—

Where rippling grasses gleefully rush
Across the waves of mounting earth
To dance with lilting,
Playful tread,
Between the savage crags of cobalt ice
That bend their Mountain arms
To fold the land in their Embrace—

Where wind and sun and shadow Breathe
Through tumbling,
Trembling,
Giggling
Leaves,
That wrestle in the steady limbs
Of sunbeam spattered, dappled Trees—

Where streams of light seep through
The shadowed veins of stony brooks
And mingle
In the silken waves
Of lapping ponds
That slip beneath the snow-
Tipped Wings of my resting Soul, before it lifts in
flight—

There—my heart begins to breathe, "I'm home."

www.ingramcontent.com/pod-product-compliance
Lightning Source LLC
Chambersburg PA
CBHW060543030426
42337CB00021B/4406